Belly Buttons
&
Broken Hearts

A 30-Day Shock and Awe Devotional

By Cyle Young

Praise for
Belly Buttons and Broken Hearts

Communicating with youth today requires a mixture of humor, fresh insight into scriptural truth, and relevant words. Cyle Young accomplishes this in *Belly Buttons and Broken Hearts.* The subtitle "a shock and awe devotional" foretells the mix of humorous stories with insight that will challenge those reading the devotions to a higher commitment to Jesus. This is a book well worth reading and distributing to your entire youth group.

~ Grant Edwards
Senior Pastor
Fellowship Christian Church, Springfield, Ohio
author of *Swimming Lessons*

Learning from other Christians is an important part to growing as a follower of Christ. Learning from tried and tested Christians, like Cyle Young, is a must. Cyle brings his large living experiences and insights into Scripture together in *Belly Buttons and Broken Hearts.* He also relates well to readers of all ages—pre-teen, teenager, and young adult. Buy it. Read it. Pass it on so that others can learn from God's Word and a forgiven follower of Jesus, the King.

~ Marty Sweeney
Executive Director
Matthias Media Ministries

BELLY BUTTONS AND BROKEN HEARTS: A 30-DAY SHOCK
AND AWE DEVOTIONAL
by Cyle Young
Published by Lighthouse Publishing of the Carolinas
2333 Barton Oaks Dr., Raleigh, NC, 27614

ISBN: 978-1-938499-97-5
Copyright © 2013 by Cyle Young
Cover design by Ted Ruybal, www.wisdomhousebooks.com
Book design by Reality Info Systems, www.realityinfo.com

Available in print from your local bookstore, online, or from the
publisher at: www.lighthousepublishingofthecarolinas.com

For more information on this book and the author visit:
www.cyleyoung.com

Library of Congress Cataloging-in-Publication Data:Young, Cyle.
Belly Buttons and Broken Hearts / Cyle Young 1st ed.

Printed in the United States of America

Lighthouse Publishing
of the Carolinas
www.lighthousepublishingofthecarolinas.com

Table of Contents

I dedicate this book to all the people who may be mad at me for how I portray them in my stories. No harm intended! Sorry!

Really sorry!

Disclaimer

These devotions are based upon events from my life. They are the truth as I know it to be. People I've referred to in my stories may have different memories of each story or situation than I do. They're wrong—just kidding! Over time, our minds can change what we remember to be true. Our minds may exaggerate actions, consequences, or emotions. So, these are my thoughts and my memories as I remember them. Enjoy!

Belly Buttons

Day 1

My Dog Ate My Homework

*And He said, "Who told you that you were
naked? Have you eaten from the tree of which I
commanded you not to eat?"
The man said, "The woman whom You gave to
be with me, she gave me from the tree, and I
ate."*

Genesis 3:11-12

Excuses are like...bellybuttons. Shame on you if
you were thinking something else, *butt* seriously,
everyone has a bellybutton. Or do they? A good
argument can be made that Adam and Eve didn't have
bellybuttons, but they sure had excuses.

First, the bellybuttons. Adam and Eve were never
born, and you get a bellybutton from your umbilical
cord. So, one could assume that since Adam and Eve
were never born, they never had an umbilical cord.
And thus, they never had bellybuttons.

But they had excuses. God came to talk to them
after they sinned for the first time, and what does
Adam do? He gives an excuse. Adam points to Eve,
and of course Eve then points to the snake. I bet you
can relate to that scenario at least once in your life.

Maybe you busted the neighbor's window while playing baseball outside and the neighbor comes looking for the culprit, only to find everyone pointing at everyone else.

Living Large:

Everyone has made excuses in their lives. The Bible is full of excuses why people weren't doing what they were supposed to. The problem with excuses is that they keep us away from greatness. Especially when we make excuses about why we aren't spending time with God, at church or through prayer and reading His word, and we become separated from Him.

In the Garden of Eden, God came to spend time with Adam and Eve, and because of their shame, they made excuses. God came to see them, and they hid. Not only did they hide in the bushes, but they hid their hearts from God. They couldn't be honest about why they weren't able to spend time with God, so they made excuses.

What excuses are you giving God? Are you too busy? Too tired? Too poor? Maybe it's too boring to spend time with Him. Maybe the real answer is that you haven't set God as a high priority in your life, and instead of admitting that, you make excuses.

You make God a priority when you choose God

over worldly things, like when you choose to read your Bible over playing video games or when you choose to leave a sports practice early so you can attend youth group. These decisions reveal God as a priority in your life. Choose to make God the priority of your life today.

Day 2

Aliens! Run!

"You are My servant,
I have chosen you and not rejected you.
Do not fear, for I am with you;
Do not anxiously look about you, for I am your
God.
I will strengthen you, surely I will help you,
Surely I will uphold you with My righteous
right hand."

Isaiah 41:9-10

Ever wonder about the crazy things that we fear in life? Some people fear spiders or snakes. Others fear speaking in public or answering the phone. Some people have normal fears that are shared by a large segment of the population; others, like me, fear strange things.

I've been known to have a vivid imagination. A vivid imagination can intensify the fears that we already possess. My imagination magnifies some of my fears. I fear heights, snakes, being in a plane while it is crashing, sharks, and the Devil. (I'll explain that one later.) I also have a big fear of aliens. Yes, that's right—aliens.

One night, when I was in high school, I saw an

alien spaceship flying low outside my house. What did a huge 225-pound football player do? I ran into my mom and dad's room to make sure they would be taken first. That's right. I know. I know. You're thinking, "What a ... smart move." I agree! My plan, of course, was that my parents would barter with the aliens and offer themselves so that I would be left behind and probe free. Well, I'm glad to tell you we made it.

You see, my issue of fearing aliens was twofold. First, I was a young teen in the United States during the heyday of alien movies. Second, I spent too much time reading books and watching movies. I spent more time with things that caused fear than I did with the Bible. I focused on fear and it overran my thoughts.

Living Large:

God doesn't want us to let fear control us. God promises to strengthen and uphold us. It's amazing to think that God placed "do not fear" in the Bible 365 times, one for each day of each year of our lives. God wants us to look to Him for our strength, and He will hold us up so we can face our fears.

What fears are holding you back? What fears do you need to give over to God? What secret fears do you need to bring out into the open? Write them down and pray over them, asking God to remove these fears from your heart.

Just in case you're wondering how I'm doing with

my fear of aliens, let me put it this way: If I'm walking through the woods one night and E.T. pops out with his glowing heart and a bag of Reese's Pieces, and let's just say that E.T. reaches out to me with his creepy glowing finger, I don't care. I'm cracking him in the head with the nearest dead branch I can find, stealing his Reese's Pieces, and running through the woods screaming like a little girl.

Day 3

Kazaam

*Zaccheus was trying to see who Jesus was,
and was unable because of the crowd, for he
was small in stature. So he ran on ahead and
climbed up into a sycamore tree in order to see
Him, for He was about to pass through that
way. When Jesus came to the place, He looked
up and said to him, "Zaccheus, hurry and come
down, for today I must stay at your house."*

Luke 19:3-5

Do you ever wonder why people ran to meet Jesus? Why giant crowds followed him everywhere He went? Have you ever thought that some of the people in the Bible were just absolutely crazy, like Zaccheus in the tree or the four dudes that cut the hole in the roof?

Well, I have. What I've come to realize is that we can all be a little crazy when we see someone famous who we really admire. It's part of being human, I think.

Over the years, I've known or met lots of famous people. I met former President Clinton at the White House, and I played college football with some of today's biggest NFL stars. There was one day, though, when I became one of those crazy people who would do anything to meet someone famous.

We were at the Rose Bowl in 1997, playing for the National Championship. All of the players from both teams got to do fun, local activities; we got to live the high life for a few days.

One night, our entire team went to a Lakers game. We went down onto the court before the game and met Bill Walton. (He is a famous, former basketball player/sportscaster.) It was neat to meet him, but I wanted to meet Shaq. I devised a better plan.

Shaq was injured, so he relaxed on the bench during warm-ups. That was my shot. A few of us made our way around the arena and started down the aisle that led to the Lakers' bench. About halfway to the bench, we were stopped. One of the Lakers greeters wanted to see our tickets. We didn't have tickets for that row.

So, we told a half-truth. (I'm not saying in any way that lying is okay. I'm just telling our story.) We told the lady that we needed to get our teammates, who were seated farther down by the court, because we had to leave. Half of that was true. The other half … um … not so much. She bought it. Luckily, our team had been introduced before the game, so this lady knew who we were.

We proceeded down to the court, where we hit our next roadblock—bodyguards. You may not think someone who is seven feet tall and 300 pounds needs bodyguards, but he has them. Out of the corner of my eye, I spotted Magic Johnson seated courtside. We introduced ourselves to him. He was very gracious and wished us luck. We then asked Magic to introduce us to Shaq. He obliged and helped us get past the bodyguards. Shaq shook our hands and wished us luck in the Rose Bowl. It was great. We felt like we were on top of the world.

Living Large:

I imagine that's how Zaccheus probably felt. I know I would feel on top of the world if I saw Jesus. Have you ever felt like you were on top of the world? Has Jesus ever made you feel that way?

Make a list of the things you don't like about yourself. Then, read Psalm 139.

Day 4

Punxsutawney Phil

*For the flesh sets its desire against the Spirit,
and the Spirit against the flesh; for these are in
opposition to one another, so that you may not
do the things that you please.
But if you are led by the Spirit, you are not
under the Law.*

Galatians 5:17-18

If you have ever seen groundhogs, you know how ugly they are. They look like the offspring of a tiny bear and a beaver. They wiggle across your lawn and dive into their underground lairs. They are a nuisance animal, which means you can kill them. There are many ways to kill groundhogs: traps, smoking them out, or shooting them. Death by shotgun is probably the most common.

Sometime in my early teen years, I saw two groundhogs in my backyard. No one was home, so I took it upon myself to rid the house of these groundhogs once and for all. I got my dad's shotgun, loaded it, and headed out into the yard. I snuck around the side of the yard and climbed up into my tree house. This would allow me to bring death to the groundhogs from above, and they would never know it was coming.

I stood on the balcony and took aim. I felt the gun slowly waver in my young arms. One groundhog moved and wiggled its way underneath my position. I still had a shot, so I took it. BLAM! The recoil from the shot pushed me back a couple of feet. I didn't fall, but what I hadn't realized was that I was aiming very near my toes. A couple of inches closer and I would have shot both of my feet.

Both groundhogs darted across the yard and disappeared into their hole. Scared and a little shaken up, I went inside and immediately put the gun away. The worst part wasn't that I almost blew my feet off. It was that I missed the stupid groundhog. This was the last time I ever took my dad's gun out without his permission, and to this day, I have never killed a groundhog.

Living Large:

Have you ever taken something without someone's permission? What were the consequences? My choice could have cost me more than missing one groundhog; it could have cost me ten toes.

We always need to make sure we ask to use things. Of course, my dad would have told me that I could not use his gun. Why? He probably knew that I was clueless and might have shot myself in the foot. He would have been right.

Day 5

Magneto

*A poor yet wise lad is better than an old and
foolish king who no longer knows
how to receive instruction. For he has come out
of prison to become king,
even though he was born poor in his kingdom.*

Ecclesiastes 4:13-14

I enjoy the game of golf. I am horrible at it, but I enjoy playing the game. For any of you who want to know how bad I am at golf, let's just say if I break 100, it's a really good day. For those who don't know anything about golf, par is seventy-two and the pros hit less than that, so I am pretty bad. Nonetheless, I love the game—or at least the experience of it.

On a golf course you are "away." Away from phones, television, work, people, etc. You are surrounded by nothing but God's beautiful nature and the occasional errant golf ball. There's nothing like standing on a golf course, the sun beating down on you, green grass under your feet, listening to birds chirping and leaves rustling. I think sometimes that the Garden of Eden had many similarities to a golf course.

Golf is a game of accuracy, and that is my big problem with it. When I play golf, it seems that my golf balls are magnetically attracted to trees and water. I can hit a golf ball, and if there is one tiny little tree in the middle of an expanse of green grass the size of Texas, my ball will hit that stinking tree. It's the same with water hazards on a course. My balls will find the tiniest bit of water on every hole.

It's easy to play golf with me. All you do is let me tee off and then wait about three seconds for the "thwack" of the ball hitting the tree or the "sploosh" of the ball splashing into the water. After that, you just drive the cart in that direction. I am so talented at golf that I have been able to hit a tree and put the ball in the water in the same shot.

You may feel the same way about areas of your life. You may feel that bad things, events, people, or circumstances are "magnetically" attracted to you. Many times, a lot of it boils down to trying to live your life without the help, advice, or counsel of others.

I have never taken golf lessons. Rather, I have never sought after or heeded the wise counsel of a PGA-certified golf instructor. That's probably why I am not too good at golf. But, this year for Christmas, I got golf lessons. So as of this spring, hopefully I won't stink as bad.

Living Large:

If you feel like you suck at some area of your life, maybe it's time to seek wise counsel. Of course, the

Bible is the wisest counsel of all, but we have also been blessed with parents, pastors, and other godly people who we can ask for advice. Life is meant to be lived together in community, and we were meant to seek the advice of elders. We were never meant to find our own path and do everything by ourselves.

Through my upcoming golf lessons, I'm not going to become a great golfer overnight, but it's a beginning. And, through seeking advice, your life won't change dramatically overnight, but it's the start of a journey that will hopefully allow you to handle all of life's magnetic craziness.

Who can you turn to for advice in your life? What decisions are you facing right now that you should ask someone for wisdom on handling them?

Find a brother, sister, parent, or pastor and ask them to share their godly wisdom with you.

Day 6

Ring the Buoy Bell

*Because that which is known about God is
evident within them; for God made it evident
to them. For since the creation of the world
His invisible attributes, His eternal power
and divine nature, have been clearly seen, being
understood through what has been made,
so that they are without excuse.*

Romans 1:19-20

If you have ever thought that you are God's gift to man/womankind, then I have a challenge for you. Go to a beach somewhere and stand out in the breaking waves on a really windy day. Choose a day when the waves are at least eight feet high. While you're standing there, don't move. Resist the ocean. Resist the waves.

You will fail miserably. The ocean will beat and batter you. The waves will pound you into the sand. You won't be able to stand still. The harder you fight against the ocean, the more tired you will get. And, before you know it, you will be hundreds of yards down the shore from where you started. What will you learn? You will learn that you aren't God's gift to the world. (Oh, and by the way, if you can't swim, don't accept this challenge.)

There is a second part to this challenge. After you learn this, go to the Bible and start reading through it. You will learn that Jesus was God's gift to the world and that the world was God's gift to us. The world doesn't need any of us in particular; it doesn't revolve around any of us. It has been here a long time before us and will exist a long time after us.

You might now be asking, "Well, what do we do with this gift?" What do you do with any gift? You play with it, enjoy it, take care of it, and are proud of it.

How do you do that? Easy. Lie on a beach and enjoy the sun. Go skiing. Visit the Grand Canyon or Angel Falls. Don't litter, and share with people the great beauties that you have seen on this earth.

Living Large:

The Bible says that God is evident in all of creation, to all people. Where have you seen evidence of God in creation? Are there people in whom you see evidence of God's love? Have you ever been somewhere that proves to you that God must be real?

Share with people where you see evidence of God in the beauty of this earth. When you share, do it with joy and excitement. Hopefully, you will allow someone's eyes to be opened to our loving God, who is evident every day in this wonderful world.

Day 7

Cold-Hearted Snake

After these things the word of the Lord came to
Abram in a vision, saying,
"Do not fear, Abram,
I am a shield to you;
Your reward shall be very great."

Genesis 15:1

When I was a young boy, I loved to pretend I was a great warrior who could save the world by myself, sort of like Rambo. I would get a green army sack, toss it over my arm, and head off to fight the great battles that I always won. I never left home without my trusty rifle (which was actually one of my mom's wooden twirling rifles, but it looked real). When I went out on these great adventures, I killed countless numbers of the enemy, saved the prisoners, and became the hero.

A particularly memorable battle occurred one sunny, autumn day. I slowly crept through the jungle (the fields behind my house). As I crept, I massacred the enemy horde I was assaulting. I advanced on their encampment and steadily made my way down the trail, when there, at the bend, I saw an unfamiliar foe. A foe so terrifying that I ran, screaming like a banshee. Between my panting and screaming, I could hear my foe chasing me, rustling the leaves behind me as it relentlessly pursued me. I broke from the field to see my father working in the yard. I screamed to warn him, "Snake! Snake! It's chasing me!" Seeing my panic, he panicked and darted to the back deck, where we both hopped to safety. Then, we looked for the snake.

There was no snake. I explained to him that I thought I saw a "racer," which is a really fast snake in Ohio. Racers have been known to chase their prey. I was sure that the racer had chased me all the way home. But, we couldn't find it. The terrifying foe that had defeated this great warrior was nowhere to be found. I came to the realization that my foe wasn't the snake. My true foe was my overwhelming fear. My *fear* of the snake caused me to run all the way home, not the racer (which I later figured out was a harmless garter snake).

Living Large:

In the Bible, God promises to shield us. Does that mean if the snake had tried to bite me that God would have stopped it? He could, but I doubt it. In this case, it means that God will protect our minds so we can remain focused and calm, not paralyzed by our fears. He will shield us from the true damage of our fears—apathy.

What fears have you let paralyze you? What fears have you let control who you are and who you can become? Embrace those fears by placing yourself in situations that you must rely on God—and God alone—to help you conquer those fears.

Day 8

I Would Walk 500 Miles

*So he got up and came to his father. But while
he was still a long way off, his father saw him
and felt compassion for him, and ran and
embraced him and kissed him.*

Luke 15:20

When I was in junior high, I ran away from
home. It was more like *walked away* from
home. I should probably clarify that in reality I never
intended to leave home for a long period of time. I
was just trying to make a point to my parents. There
were many times I had threatened to run away, and
I pretended to pack my bags for the trip. But, there
was only one time that I actually wanted to make my
parents really worry.

I don't remember what I was upset about, but one
night I packed and took off. I left home and headed
out into the fields behind my house. And no, my
parents did not follow me; I don't think they thought
I was going to run away. But I did.

It was early evening when I left and it was getting
dark quickly, so I made camp. Camp for me was a
couple of thin blankets and a pillow.

I had a few problems with my wonderful running

away plan. It was fall, and I didn't bring anything I needed. The ground was cold. If you have ever lain on cold ground, then you know it's really cold. I also didn't realize that when night hits, it gets even colder. My two blankets weren't cutting it. I was freezing.

I started to question my plan. I was only going to spend one night out; just enough so I could get a glorious welcome, like the prodigal son, when I returned home. I wanted my parents to be so happy that I decided to come back. I wanted to be welcomed with a feast. But, I was really cold. I decided that a couple of hours would be enough time to make them miss me, and I returned home, hoping for my welcome.

When I got home, there was no welcome, no happiness, no feast, and there were no people. My parents were in their room, with the door shut. My plan had failed. Cold and disheveled, I went to bed.

Living Large:

Have you ever wanted to run away from something? Maybe a job, home, or school? From my experience, it's a dumb idea. We gain so much maturity and knowledge when we battle through life's struggles instead of running away.

I challenge you: if you would love to run away from something in your life, don't. Jonah ran away and a giant fish swallowed him. Instead, ask God to give you the strength and courage to battle through it.

Day 9

Killa from Manilla

"The one who desires life, to love and see good days, must keep his tongue from evil and his lips from speaking deceit."

1 Peter 3:10

In high school, I was a pretty good wrestler. It was my favorite sport, and I won many titles and awards. My ultimate achievement was becoming an All-American. What I enjoyed most about wrestling was the closeness of my team and our families.

If you have never been to a wrestling match, you haven't truly lived. Here's a quick synopsis: Picture having your butt attached to a hard, plastic bleacher for two full days while you watch high school kids of various shapes and sizes beating the tar out of each other.

There were a couple of hours in between our matches, so we had to keep ourselves entertained. We joked around, played cards, and hung out with each other's families. One time, I talked with some of the parents as we sized up my next match. Jokingly, I said, "I'm gonna kill this kid." As we looked him over, we all agreed. He wasn't very muscular, and he didn't appear to be the most coordinated wrestler.

A short while later, I faced the uncoordinated kid. I quickly dominated him with a side headlock. A side headlock is not something you want to be in; basically, your face is shoved tight into someone else's sweaty, stinky armpit, and it's really hard to breathe. After I got this kid into a side headlock, I slammed him onto his back. I had his head shoved deep into my armpit and all of my 240 pounds pressed hard against his chest. The match would be over momentarily.

Then, he went limp. It felt as though I was holding a rag doll. A second later, he started to shake. He shook violently, his sweaty body flailing on the mat. His coaches ran to him, yelling for a medic.

I stood up and looked at my parents. They looked shocked, and I went pale. I killed him! That was the first thing that came to my mind. I killed him! I knew our whole section of parents was thinking the same thing. *Cyle killed him!* I didn't know what to do.

Luckily, one of their coaches saw my pale face and came over to explain that this kid was a diabetic and that this had happened before. Whew! I was relieved; I wasn't a murderer.

After we found out the kid was all right, the incident became a big joke—one of those humorous events that you can later laugh about. There was a huge life lesson to be learned from all of this: be careful what you say, it might come true.

Living Large:

Have you ever said anything that you wished you could take back? Have you ever said anything nasty or vile, and it came true? We must guard our words carefully and be positive with our speech.

Day 10

Whoa, Silver!

But Jonah rose up to flee to Tarshish from the
presence of the Lord... And the Lord
appointed a great fish to swallow Jonah, and
Jonah was in the stomach
of the fish three days and three nights.

Jonah 1:3, 17

Horseback riding is a painful way to enjoy nature and can sometimes be as thrilling as a small rollercoaster. Now, I'm a big fellow. When I go horseback riding, I can sense all the horses in the stalls praying that I don't get on their back.

I took a mentoring group to a horse-riding facility in Ohio. It was the first time many of them had ever ridden a horse. When we got to the facility, they started giving our group their horses. My kids were all excited as they were taken to the beautiful brown and black quarter horses that they would be riding. The farmhands took each teen, walked them down the horse stall, and gave them their horse. I, of course, was last. I eagerly awaited my turn to be led to a horse.

As the riding instructor came up to lead me, I followed her to the barn. She looked at me and said that my horse wasn't in the stalls. She told me to go over to the loading platform. The loading platform was six feet high and had steps to the top. I stood on top of the platform and waited. The instructor returned with a horse the size of a Sherman tank. It made all the other horses look like pygmy horses! I mounted my tank, and while I towered above everyone else, we headed out onto the trails.

Let me give you a little advice about riding a horse. Never fart on a horse that you are riding. It is a really BAD idea. We'd been riding for a while when I had the urge to pass gas. I had nowhere to go, since I was on the horse. I rose up a little bit in my saddle so I wouldn't make any noise and call attention to myself, and I let it rip.

My horse bucked up on its two back legs and neighed violently. I thought this tank-of-a-horse was going to throw me off and kill me. My life flashed before my eyes, and I thought, "Great. I'm finally going to make the *Guinness Book of World Records*, but I'm going to make it as the only man ever killed for farting on a horse."

You see, when I raised up, I didn't raise myself high enough. Instead of quietly passing gas, my butt turned into a tuba. Violent tremors sprang forth from my tuba, rattling the horse's saddle and freaking him out.

Fortunately, I didn't get killed and the horse settled down, but I learned that we must be careful of decisions we make. They may have unforeseen consequences. Take, for example, Jonah: he thought he would be safe by not going to Nineveh to preach. I am sure that, while sitting in the belly of a giant fish, he realized his previous decision was unwise.

Living Large:

I would ask if you have ever farted on a horse, but I know only a moron would do that. Think of one unwise choice that you have made. How could you have made a better, wiser decision? What can you learn from that decision that will help you make sure you don't repeat it?

Always take into account what consequences may result from your actions. Making wise choices will save you much grief in life and might keep you from getting bucked off a horse.

Day 11

We All Live in a Yellow Submarine

Listen to counsel and accept discipline,
That you may be wise the rest of your days.

Proverbs 19:20

I'm a big guy. I have routinely weighed around three bills since I left college. For those of you who don't know fat-guy lingo, that's 300 pounds. Even though I'm a big guy, I still love to do skinny guy stuff. I love all kinds of sports and crazy activities. Some examples include snowboarding, skiing, surfing, etc.

My wife and I decided to go wind surfing when we were on vacation in Kill Devil Hills, North Carolina. The wind is steady year-round in North Carolina, so it's a good place to do so. I have always seen those beautiful pictures of windsurfers skimming across the water with their colorful sails. It sounded like fun, so we tried it.

We had to rent equipment and take training classes. My wife, Patty, got up on her board with ease and was zooming around on the water. I, on the other hand, had an entirely different story. I got up on my board and looked like those pictures you see on the news of a half-submerged raft full of refugees trying to get to America. My boat was doing more wind submarining than wind surfing. I swear, if I would have taken the sail off and just stood on the board, the entire east coast of North Carolina would have come to Jesus. They would have thought I was a prophet walking on water.

The whole time I struggled with wind surfing, Patty sailed around me, laughing. I know what you're thinking, and you're right. *She's mean.* Just kidding.

Besides the board, there is one other important part of windsurfing. It's the sail. The wind is supposed to push you. The key words are *supposed to*. I wasn't going anywhere. I was just bobbin' up and down, up and down. I imagine if an F5 hurricane came through, I may have gotten some movement.

Let me give you a little piece of advice: If you are a big person, save your money. Don't windsurf. They really should advertise a weight limit.

All in all, we had a lot of fun that day. Patty windsurfed, and I ... practiced being a buoy. Would I ever go windsurfing again? In a heartbeat. After I lose some weight!

Living Large:

Ever think something was going to be fun only to find out you didn't really understand what you were getting into? Ministry can be a lot like that. You start out on fire for God and want to go out and serve. Next thing you know, you're bobbing in the water, so to speak.

Sometimes we need to step back a little and prepare ourselves for ministry, just like I need to step back and lose a little weight before I go windsurfing again. Ask someone to show you how to be effective in ministry. Seek wise counsel and advice. The more you know what you're getting into, the better prepared you'll be for ministry successes and failures.

Day 12

George of the Jungle

But the wisdom from above is first pure, then
peaceable, gentle, reasonable,
full of mercy and good fruits, unwavering,
without hypocrisy.

James 3:17

Ever done something that you were told not to do? Sure you have; we all have. It's part of growing up, and it rarely ever turns out well.

I was staying at my best friend Andy's house when I was in junior high. His dad was an umpire, so we went to the ball field while he called a game. Andy's mom specifically told us not to play with sticks in the woods adjacent to the ball field, because we could get hurt and no one was there to watch us.

That's the last thing you should tell two junior high boys. We went straight into the woods and played with old pine tree limbs that made perfect swords.

We swung the swords wildly like two Jedi in a light saber duel. With each hit, we swung harder and harder till … "crack," my sword broke. To my horror, when the stick broke it hit Andy dead between the eyes, and it hit him hard. He dropped to the ground like a sack of potatoes. By the time I looked at him and realized what happened, he had a bulbous, baseball-sized welt protruding from his forehead right between his eyes. We both knew that we were in a lot of trouble.

This was my first night with him, and I was staying all week. For sure, I was going to get sent home for this, and we couldn't let that happen. So, we made a pact. We decided to tell Andy's mom that he ran into a tree as I was chasing him. That way, neither of us would get into any trouble. We knew we couldn't get into a lot of trouble for an *accident*.

We went to tell Andy's mom. The moment she looked at her son, she was horrified. We spat out our story, and she bought it. We hurried to the car and rushed to the hospital. Andy had a mild concussion, and we had to wake him every hour that night. We had to ask him questions to make sure he didn't have any brain trauma. It was horrible.

We felt so bad and so guilty. You're probably wondering if we ever told his mom the truth. The answer is yes. About fifteen years later I told her— during my toast at Andy's wedding. It was hilarious, because so much time had passed. But, I don't advise lying; the guilt will follow you for a long time. In our case, fifteen years!

Living Large:

The Bible is full of advice to keep us safe. God knew we wouldn't listen all the time. He gave us a great reminder that we can constantly refer back to when we try to do our own thing, mess up, and make mistakes. When we read the Bible and do what it says, God's Word can save us from an enormous amount of heartache and grief by steering us clear of bad choices.

As a person that loves God, it is imperative to spend time in his word—daily. Without the knowledge of the Bible, we won't know and understand God's guidance in our lives.

Do you read your Bible every day? If not, why? Create a plan to read the Bible daily.

I am a dump-a-day kinda guy—yes, that means I poop once each day. I keep a devotional and Bible under the sink in the bathroom so I can read them whenever I'm droppin' a deuce. Find a time in your day that you can set aside to read the Bible, even if it's in the bathroom.

Day 13

Devil's Gonna Getcha!

*"O Jacob My servant, do not fear," declares the
Lord, "For I am with you."*

Jeremiah 46:28

I used to be afraid of the Devil. Not figuratively, but *literally*. I thought the Devil was going to grab me and drag me to hell. I can remember watching TV in our dark basement. I would be watching some show, normally about aliens or something scary, and I would be worried that the Devil was going to reach over the exposed back of our L-shaped couch. It would be from the darkness of the void behind my couch that the Devil's attack would come.

Luckily, I'm smarter than the Devil, and I know a thing or two. Well, actually, just two. I know that to be protected from a surprise attack from the Devil, you can cover yourself up with a warm blanket. He never attacked while I was covered up.

The other thing that I know helped me avoid the Devil when I was most exposed.

The most dangerous part of watching TV in my dark basement was going to bed. For starters, I had to leave the protection of the blanket. Then, I had to turn off the TV. Total darkness! Nothing was scarier or more dangerous. Thankfully, I was smart enough to devise a strategy. I would turn the TV off with the remote as I sprinted from the couch and up the stairs. I would then throw the remote down onto the couch. Pure genius, I know. This plan kept me alive throughout years of late-night TV watching.

Fortunately, I later learned that the Devil can't attack you in a physical sense, and I got over this silly fear.

What I still *don't* know is if my parents ever figured out why all the remotes never lasted long. Could it be that most times they bounced off the couch and onto the floor? Oops!

Living Large:

We all have times when we misunderstand the Devil's impact in our lives. The Bible is clear to point out that the Devil is a great tempter and can put many obstacles in our paths to hold us back from experiencing the fullness of God's love.

What could be holding you back? Choose one thing in your life that you will overcome so you can grow closer to God.

Day 14

The 96-Ouncer

If you are slack in the day of distress,
Your strength is limited.

Proverbs 24:10

I once ate seven pounds of prime rib in one sitting. Let me clarify. When I say seven pounds, I mean the meat was seven pounds. I also had to eat all of the sides, which included seven heaping sides of mashed potatoes and vegetables.

You are probably wondering why any sane person would eat this much in one sitting. (Most people do.) The simple answer is peer pressure. I wanted to be cool. And what could make a guy any cooler than eating an enormously fattening amount of food? Nothing!

We live in a world where the hotdog-eating championship is world-televised. Nowadays, food-eating champions are celebrities. I thought that eating an enormous amount of food would vault my popularity to a crazy level. People would know me as the guy that ate all the meat. I thought they would know me all over the world.

As fun as my fame was from eating all that meat,

I realized it was a truly stupid thing to do. Especially since there are starving people all over the world, and I gorged myself on all that meat. It was a stupid idea, because my fame didn't last. It came and went. Soon, people would forget my name and what I did. And for all that fame, I risked my health. I could have had serious consequences from eating all that food. It was risky and dumb.

So, why did I really do it? Well, I was at a football bowl game, and a local restaurant had an eating contest between the two teams that were playing in the game. I wanted to make sure my team won. Some upperclassmen pressured me and encouraged me to keep going, so I did. I stuffed myself. I didn't want to lose face as a freshman in front of the older guys.

The funny thing is that I cannot remember whether we won the competition that year or not. In the long run, it wasn't important. All I remember is that I ate a lot of meat, felt like I was stuffed for days, and got myself into a lot of trouble with my coach.

Living Large:

Have you ever let peer pressure get you to do something stupid or immoral? Have you ever wanted to look cool in front of somebody or a group of people and ended up doing something embarrassing? The great thing is we don't have to try to impress God; He loves us just as we are.

Next time you're about to let other people pressure you, think about the consequences.

And if you ever think about trying to duplicate my seven-pound feat, let me give you one little tidbit of advice: with seven pounds of meat comes seven pounds of constipation.

Day 15

Mission Impossible

For nothing will be impossible with God.

Luke 1:37

I realized that nothing is impossible while I wrestled in high school. I wrestled in a tournament at West Liberty High School. It was our sectional meet, which is the first of three meets you have to get through to become state champion. I wasn't worried about any of my competition at sectionals, so I relaxed, won my matches, and had a good time.

My first match was against the weakest opponent at the tournament. He looked goofy and probably shouldn't have been a wrestler. Somebody along the way should have told him to try a different sport.

Before the match, I sized up my opponent. He looked really uncoordinated. Jokingly, I told our parents' section, "I'm gonna pin this kid in ten seconds!"

Pinning someone in ten seconds is difficult. You have to get them from their feet to their back and hold their shoulders firmly to the mat for nearly a whole second.

I was trying to get a laugh by saying this and I did.

A little while later, the match began. I grabbed him

and threw him to the mat like a limp rag. I threw all my weight into him to hold him down, and SMACK! The referee hit the mat, signaling that the match was over.

I stood up and looked at the clock: nine seconds. My jaw hit the floor. I looked up into the crowd and our fans were laughing. They couldn't believe it either. I had actually pinned the guy in less than ten seconds. It was at this moment when I realized that nothing is impossible.

Living Large:

I love that the Bible promises nothing is impossible with God. No matter how bad life gets or feels we can still conquer anything with God. I hope that you will have an experience like mine. I hope something amazing will happen in your life to lead you to realize that nothing is impossible, especially when you have God on your side.

Broken Hearts

Day 16

Tough as Nails

... nor height, nor depth, nor any other created
thing, will be able to separate us from
the love of God, which is in Christ Jesus our
Lord.

Romans 8:39

If anyone knows about "tough love" in this world, then it definitely has got to be me. I'm not saying that tough love is bad. On the contrary, I believe it's extremely effective when used properly.

My parents and I got into a huge argument over who-knows-what. We were screaming and yelling, and I probably threatened to run away. My parents probably threatened to whip me. Instead, they suddenly began packing a bag for me. Were they really going to let me run away *and* pack for me too? I wish that was the case. The next thing I heard sent me on a horrific journey that some may say changed my life, while therapists may say it scarred me forever.

"You're going to go to the Oesterlen Home," they said.

"Whatever," I yelled back.

The Oesterlen Home is our local home for troubled teens. It's not a place you want to live at voluntarily, but they do have a nice pool and gym. Of course, I didn't believe my parents were going to take me there. But, I decided to play their little game. I would go.

They packed me up, and we got into the van. About five minutes later, we were on the road outside of Oesterlen. My dad told me to get out. He even walked around the side of the van and opened the door. I was freaking out. These crazy people were serious.

I screamed and cried, "I'm not getting out!" It was at that point that I apologized for anything and everything I had ever done wrong. They must have believed me, because they let me go home.

It took me a while to learn that you can't just drop your kids off at Oesterlen. There are proper channels and paperwork. But I have to say, my parents' tough-love scare tactic worked.

Living Large:

Isn't it great that when we act really bad or spoiled, God doesn't try to get rid of us or give us away? He loves us even when we are at our worst. Next time you act badly or spoiled, remember that God still loves you, even though He doesn't like your behavior.

I occasionally drive by the Oesterlen Home now. I slow down so I can remember this wonderful moment in my past. Or, it could be that I slow down because I start twitching…

Day 17

Burn, Baby, Burn!

"But if your enemy is hungry, feed him, and if
he is thirsty, give him a drink;
for in so doing you will heap burning coals on
his head."

Romans 12:20

You have never really experienced excitement in life until you drive across an overpass bridge, and as you reach the crest of the hill, where you can just see the other side, you notice your mailbox is in flames.

Early in my high school career, that was one of my wonderful experiences. As we pulled up to our house, a car was pulled over and someone was by the mailbox. My dad pulled into our yard, and it was on. We were going to hand this guy a beat down.

We found out he and his girlfriend were driving by, and they were putting out the fire. Once we extinguished the fire, we had to decipher what had happened. (Just in case you're wondering, mailboxes do not catch fire spontaneously; it's okay to get your mail.)

What happened was, some not-so-bright older

students came over that Saturday night and lit our mailbox on fire. These guys didn't like my older brother, so to show him, they decided to burn our mailbox down. I knew all these guys, and none of them were smart. You see, burning someone's mailbox down is a double felony. Arson is one felony, and destroying a mailbox is another.

These teenagers could have faced some serious jail time. Instead of calling the police, my mom skipped church on Sunday morning and went to the houses of all the students involved. She told them and their parents that we would not call the police if they all came over and put up a new mailbox.

So, we threw a pizza party and they all came over and we got a new mailbox. I guess I shouldn't say party, because the air was thick with tension.

I have to say, my mother's attempt to show forgiveness and love to these boys worked for a few of them. For the others, it just intensified their hatred and disgust for my brother and my family.

Living Large:

In life, people will not always respond to your grace and love the way that you hope they will. That doesn't mean we shouldn't keep trying. One of those boys was a really close friend of my brother, who betrayed that friendship by helping to burn down our mailbox. My mother's grace helped to restore that friendship and provided much-needed forgiveness in their lives.

Have you ever been hurt by someone who was close to you? You can show grace to the people in your life who have harmed you or hurt you. The first step is to forgive them and then love them as Christ loves us.

Day 18

Timber!

*All things indeed are clean, but they are evil
for the man who eats and gives offense. It is
good not to eat meat or to drink wine, or to do
anything by which your brother stumbles.*

Romans 14:20b-21

At least once in your life, you've probably tried to trip someone. Hopefully, it was just for fun and you didn't want to hurt or embarrass that person. I will admit to tripping one or two … or fifty people in my life. I will add that I have never tripped a stranger, at least not on purpose.

You know what I'm talking about when I say tripping. Someone is walking in front of you, and you get this sudden urge to stick your foot in between theirs and watch them go crashing down. Of course, for a moment, you act concerned (when really you're just making sure they aren't seriously hurt), and then you bust out laughing. We laugh at the embarrassed person sprawled out on the floor as they scramble to get up as fast as possible, so they can chase us and retaliate with a wedgie or a sloppy wet willy. Then, both people end up laughing hysterically, hopefully.

Living Large:

Causing someone to stumble in his or her walk
with Christ is no laughing matter. The Bible is clear
that we need to live our lives in ways that will help
people know God better, not cause them to fall.

How do we cause people to stumble? It's simple:
we do things in our lives that people see, and it either
offends the person or leads them into sin. Some
areas that Christians can be huge stumbling blocks
for others are: swearing, drinking, smoking, gossip,
attitude, sexual temptation, and many more.

We don't realize how important our thoughts and
actions are. By participating in these lifestyle choices,
we validate them for others. Someone might look at
your life and say, "So-and-so swears and is a Christian,
so I can too," or "So-and-so drinks, so I can too."

The problem is that if a person sees you drink or
swear and then begins or continues to do those things
in their life, and eventually they fall away from God
because of it, you are the cause. You are the stumbling
block that helped drive a wedge between them and
God. It's like a person is heading toward Jesus, and you
stick your foot out and trip them so they don't make it
to Him. As Christians, we need to live lives of purity
in all areas so that those around us are encouraged
by our Christian walks, not tripped up and separated
from God.

What actions, thoughts, or attitudes in your life

may be causing others to stumble? Pick one of the areas that you struggle with and begin working to correct that behavior in your life. For example, if you struggle with swearing, create a swear jar and place a dollar in the jar every time you swear. Once you fill the jar (hopefully it's not soon), donate the money to a charity.

Day 19

Duh-duh. Duh-duh.

*For certain persons have crept in unnoticed,
those who were long beforehand marked
out for this condemnation, ungodly persons who
turn the grace of our God into
licentiousness and deny our only Master and
Lord, Jesus Christ.*

Jude 1:4

Surfing is a sport that everybody should try at least once in their lifetime. I went surfing for the first time at the age of twenty-seven. I enjoyed it a lot. There is something exciting about being in the ocean and riding the waves. I will say that I wasn't a natural surfer, but I did get up on the board and catch a couple waves.

I noticed an interesting thing while I was surfing. While you are waiting for your wave, which can take awhile, you lay or sit on your board and let your feet dangle in the ocean. This seemed normal to everyone else, but to me it reminded me of ... how do I say it? Bait! No wonder surfers get bit. Eventually, if you cast long enough, some fish is going to bite the worm. Duh!

Of course, I wasn't going be some shark's worm. While I waited for the wave, I laid with all of my body on the board, out of the water. This severely lessened my chances of being shark bait but increased my chances of being made fun of. In my opinion, getting laughed at is much better than having half a leg.

Living Large:

My surfing experience, in many ways, relates to our daily lives. There are many times as Christians when we dangle ourselves out into the world of sharks, like bait. It may be hanging out at clubs or going to wild parties or fooling around with your boyfriend of girlfriend. And just like with surfing, if you dangle yourself out there long enough, you're going to get bit. You may slip and start drinking, go too far sexually, or take drugs.

Instead, we need to lead wholesome lives that attract others to God. We need to stop hanging out in the attractive places of the world.

Do you participate in events or activities that you know don't please God? Do you go places you shouldn't? As Christians, we need to avoid harm's way. We also need to surround ourselves with godly people in godly places. Of course, we should always befriend non-Christians. But, if all you do is spend time with people who don't know or love Jesus, it will have a bad effect on your life. Spend the majority of your time with godly people, so when you are with non-Christians, you can be a powerful witness, not a hypocrite.

Day 20

Baby Ruth

Now may our Lord Jesus Christ Himself and
God our Father, who has loved us
and given us eternal comfort and good hope by
grace, comfort and strengthen
your hearts in every good work and word.

2 Thessalonians 2:16-17

When I was younger, I was extremely backward and shy around girls my age. But, like most other junior high boys, I wanted a girlfriend. I have many "memorable" experiences from asking girls out during junior high.

In sixth grade, I had a huge crush on this girl. She was gorgeous and smart. She had long, blond hair and a pretty smile. We both had last names near the end of the alphabet, so we were always in homeroom together. I decided one night that I was going to call her to ask her out.

That night, my family and I were watching a movie called *The Goonies*. I didn't want my family to know that I was calling her, because if she told me no, I would be even more embarrassed.

During the movie, I pretended to go to the bathroom. I headed upstairs to my brother's room;

he had a phone in there. I picked up the phone and froze. I couldn't dial. My heart raced and my palms got sweaty. I put the phone down. I tried again— same result. I devised a new plan. I would pick up the phone, take a deep breath, then count to five and dial. I tried it, but I got nervous and failed. I kept trying, and finally I managed to dial the numbers. As the phone rang, I slammed it down, nervous again.

This went on for a while, until I finally found enough courage to let it keep ringing. At this point, the girl I was calling probably knew it was me from my ten-plus calls showing on her caller ID. By the time I reached her, she must have thought I was some crazed stalker.

To make my long story short, I finally got her on the phone and asked her out. She said no. The conversation lasted maybe twenty seconds total. I was devastated. I was rejected.

Living Large:

Unlike my sixth-grade crush, God doesn't reject us. He loves us. He cares for us and wants us to be in constant fellowship with him. He died for us so that we won't ever be rejected, if we'll just embrace him.

Have you ever been rejected before? Ask God to comfort you at the times you feel no one else wants you or loves you. He will.

I will add one more thing. If you are ever going

to call and ask someone out, do it while watching *The Goonies*. That crazy Sloth yelling, "HEYYY YOUUU GUYYYS" can make you forget about being rejected, at least for a little while. It worked for me!

Day 21

Holy Crap

If we confess our sins, He is faithful and
righteous to forgive us our sins
and to cleanse us from all unrighteousness.

1 John 1:9

I love dogs! Dogs truly are man's best friends. They are always happy to see you, love to cuddle, and are there for you when you are having your worst days. My wife and I have five dogs, and people think we're nuts. But, they're like children to us, our family.

As great as dogs are, there is one major downfall—scooping poop. If you have a dog, you know what I mean. It's the absolute worst thing that you have to do as a dog owner.

At my house, we use poop scoopers. I'm not one of those weird dog people that like to use a baggy and reach down with their baggy-covered hand to clean up the dog poop. I'm normal. I like to have at least a good three- to four-foot pole attached to the scooper, keeping me as far away as possible from the business end of the stick.

Scooping poop is rough. There is always an awful smell. And, when you have five dogs, it can take forever. But, the real problem with scooping is that the poop gets caked to the scooper. That's when I shake the stick until it falls off. I have to be careful, though. If I shake the stick too hard, I'll be covered in poop. I know this from experience.

I have found the best way to clean a scooper is to use a high-pressure power washer. Just spray away from your feet—again, learned from experience.

Living Large:

Our lives resemble a poop scooper in many ways. We start out as a perfect, clean, unused scooper. Then, after trying to deal with some of the crap life hands us, the poop starts sticking to us, and we can't get it off. No matter how much we shake and we try to clean it ourselves, we still can't get the poop off. It's at those times when we have to use something stronger and longer lasting to clean us. For Christians, we need to turn to Jesus.

It says in John that He will purify us and forgive us for all of the crap we've done in our lives. (No, the Bible doesn't say crap. I paraphrased the verse.) We cannot get clean without Christ's power wash. He makes us new again. After we've been made new again, we can go out into the world and share how great it is to be cleansed.

What areas of your life do you need to ask God to clean? What areas of your heart do you need to ask God to clean? Ask God to reveal the areas of your heart and life that are covered by sin, and then ask God to forgive you for those sins.

Day 22

Go Vacuum Your Room

And we know that God causes all things
to work together for good to those who love
God, to those who are called according to His
purpose. For those whom He foreknew, He also
predestined to become conformed to the image of
His Son.

Romans 8:28-29

I don't like to vacuum. Mainly because I don't like to clean, and vacuuming is cleaning. But, on occasion, I have vacuumed. Another reason I don't like to vacuum is that it's pointless. The carpet is going to get dirty again. It's a never-ending cycle, and I don't like cycles.

Also, when you're sweeping, have you ever noticed all the soft, snow-like particles flying around in the sunrays coming through the window? Do you know what that is? Dust. When you vacuum, all you are really doing is forcing all the dirt and dust back into the air. I guess the maker of the vacuum cleaner decided it's better to breathe it in than to walk on it.

After you vacuum, you have to dust, because the dust you didn't breathe in is now on your mantle, shelves, and tables. Ahh! That means more cleaning. Vacuuming is so pointless.

Living Large:

Many people all over the world feel just like a vacuum—pointless. They don't have a purpose; they don't know why they were born or what they are going to do with their lives. They haven't figured out that God has a plan and a purpose for each of us. Not only did God create us, but He also has a job for each and every one of us. We're not all going to be pastors or teachers or politicians. We each have an individual purpose, which God intended for us to carry out. There are no mistakes; God planned every one.

What do you think that God's purpose for your life is? If you don't know, talk to your parents or your pastor and ask what they think God's plan is for your life. Once you figure that out, consider what you can be doing now to reach that goal.

Day 23

Ice, Ice Baby

*Then I said, "They are only the poor, they are
foolish;
For they do not know the way of the Lord
Or the ordinance of their God."*

Jeremiah 5:4

Between high school and college, I joined
Athletes in Action, a wrestling team that took
me to Guatemala and El Salvador. It was my first trip
outside of the country, except for the time I went to
Canada.

Both countries were full of exciting new adventures
and friendly people. They were also full of immense
poverty; but for the most part, the people were happy.

One of the great advantages of being American and
traveling to third-world countries is that everything is
cheap. You can buy anything for pennies on the dollar,
literally.

We began our trip in Guatemala, where we stayed
at the Olympic Training Center. It doesn't compare to
our American Olympic complex in Colorado, by any
means.

After a hard day of practice, one of our greatest joys
was to walk outside the compound. We'd head down

toward the local street vendors to buy pop and bags of water. It was awesome. The vendors sold plastic bags of cold water for five cents. They also sold Coke in little plastic sandwich baggies with a straw for ten cents. We learned that glass bottles were so valuable that pop was only sold in baggies.

We were specifically warned not to drink anything with water in it, but we were told that pop was okay. So we drank. We would buy our little baggies of pop and ice, put our straw in them, and drink them while we walked all the way back to our compound. It was great after a long day of wrestling.

Then it began. One by one, we came down with explosive diarrhea. We all felt like leaky faucets. The worst part was that we were only a few days into a three-week tour. On top of it, we didn't have toilet paper or running water when we arrived in El Salvador. Try using receipts instead of toilet paper. It was awful. Let's just say that's the last place you want a paper cut—ouch.

Needless to say, all of us "pop" drinkers who were too dumb to realize that ice is water had diarrhea for three solid weeks until we got back to our American doctors.

Living Large:

Sometimes, we think we know what we are doing. But, in reality, the choices we make lead us down the wrong path. Sometimes that path may lead to diarrhea—or worse. The path may lead us farther away from a relationship with God.

What foolish things have you done in your life? What foolish choices have you made that affect your relationship with God? Make a list of ways that you can resist making the same foolish choices in the future.

Day 24

Legos

The earth is the Lord's, and all it contains,
The world, and those who dwell in it.

Psalm 24:1

Legos may be the best toy ever created. There are an infinite number of buildings, cars, and forts that you can build with them. I used to play with Legos—a lot. What I loved about playing with them was that I was in charge. I created their world. I created their buildings. And, I controlled their people.

In the house I grew up in, we had a room that I created entire Lego civilizations in. I named all the people and created epic battles and love stories. I had all the power, and I decided who lived, who died, and, of course, who would rescue the princess. At the end of every great battle, at least one evil villain was split in half and left with a sword, spear, saber, or axe sticking out of him. In my Lego world, evildoers always got what they deserved.

Living Large:

It is much the same in our world. God promises that in the end the Devil will pay for his crimes. He also tells us that the world we live in is His creation, and everything in it belongs to Him. Our world is full of great battles and love stories.

Did you know that you are taking place in both the greatest love story ever told and the greatest battle ever fought? The greatest battle is over our souls, and the greatest love story told is the one where Jesus dies on the cross for our sins.

You play a part in the story every day, and God allows you to choose how you want to play it. Do you truly want to embrace Jesus' love? Are you willing to fight for God so more souls join His side? Are you experiencing God's wonderful love?

As Christians, we need to experience God's power through submission. We need to submit our lives to his control.

When you wake up tomorrow, start your day by telling God that you are going to focus your day on living under His power, and strive to share Christ with other people.

Day 25

Love Stinks

*Therefore let it be known to you, brethren, that
through Him forgiveness of sins is
proclaimed to you, and through Him everyone
who believes is freed from all things,
from which you could not be freed through the
Law of Moses.*

Acts 13:38-39

The first time a girl ever told me she loved me I was at Scioto Camp in southwest Ohio.

I was in seventh or eighth grade, and I was king of the world. I had a new girlfriend. She'd been my crush for three or four years. I saw her every year at camp, and this year was my year. She was mine.

It was great, except for when she told me she loved me. It totally weirded me out. I didn't love her—at least not in that way. So, I did what every male on the face of the earth has probably done at least once in his life. I waited until we went home and never responded to any of her letters. I would read them. I just didn't respond. Out of sight—out of mind.

The problem with this strategy was that it brought a lot of guilt with it. Every letter she sent got more depressing as she begged for me to write back, and I felt guiltier. Her last letter finally read something like, *"If you don't write me back, then you never loved me at all."* So, of course I ... never wrote her back. I felt guilty about it, until one day a few years ago.

I was looking for a new job working with youth. I had applied at a youth center in her hometown. The center called me, and I had a phone interview. They placed me on speakerphone for the interview. During the interview, they mentioned that someone on their committee knew me. They told me it was the girl from camp. I almost died. I had all this guilt about how I ruined her life, and now I was back in contact with her.

The news that she was getting married relieved my guilt—phew! I didn't get the job, but I don't think the letters had anything to do with it. At least I hope they didn't.

Living Large:

Have you done something in your past that you still feel guilty about today? What can you do to correct that situation, so you don't feel guilty anymore? After you figure out how you can correct the situation, correct it. It may be as simple as saying you're sorry and asking for forgiveness.

Day 26

Crack Kills

*For You formed my inward parts; You wove me
in my mother's womb.
I will give thanks to You, for I am fearfully and
wonderfully made;
Wonderful are Your works, and my soul knows
it very well.*

Psalm 139:13-14

Have you ever laughed at someone when you've seen their butt crack hanging out of their pants? Well, shame on you. It was probably me you were laughing at. It's hard not to laugh at someone when you see plumber's butt. I have also occasionally laughed at people who are showing too much crack.

Some people have said that butt crack is pornography. Well people, if showing a little butt crack when you bend over is pornography, then I'm the biggest supplier of pornography east of the Mississippi. My crack is everywhere. To know me is to know my crack, to befriend me is to befriend my crack, and to love me is to love my crack. There is nothing we People of the Giant Crack (POTGC) can do about it. It is nature.

Let me give you some advice for the next time you

are at the grocery store, see someone grabbing an item off the bottom shelf, and they happen to show a little crack.

1. Do not yell, "Crack kills!" The last thing members of the POTGC want is to have attention called to it.

2. Do not walk up and stick a quarter in it. There is nothing more humiliating than feeling that cold steel slide between your cheeks, down your pant leg, and clang onto the floor.

3. Don't run up to the person, grab their arm, pull on it, and yell "Cha-ching!" The members of POTGC are not slot machines.

The best thing would be to casually move to the next aisle, then laugh.

Seriously, though, we all have things about us that are embarrassing. I have learned to live with the fact that every time I bend over, I'm mooning everyone. Some people have bad body odor, wet the bed, pass gas, burp loudly, have one toe that's longer than the rest, snore, or have bad breath. It's these differences and quirks that make us unique.

Living Large:

We need to learn that God created each of us to be one of a kind. Sometimes we may be embarrassed by our bodies, but it is part of life. We need to love people for who they are—quirks and all. We should not emotionally tear people apart and hurt their feelings for something they can't control or that embarrasses them, because we each have our own quirks that embarrass us.

What quirks do you have? What quirks do your friends and family have? How can you celebrate your uniqueness and respect the quirks of others? Pick a quirk that you recognize in others and begin praying that God will allow you to accept people with that quirk and recognize they are still very special to God.

Day 27

Sucker

*For the sorrow that is according to the will
of God produces a repentance without regret,
leading to salvation, but the sorrow of the world
produces death.*

2 Corinthians 7:10

Have you ever done something in life that, one second later, you wished you could take back? Life would truly be great if it came with a rewind button. I had such an experience one morning as friends and I drove to King's Island amusement park.

It was the morning after prom, and I was riding in the backseat of my friend's car with my date. He and his date were up front. It was a gorgeous May morning. The sun was shining, and the temperature was just warm enough. We had the windows halfway down so the air could cool us off. The radio was playing, and we headed toward an exciting day filled with roller coasters and water rides.

My date was my dream date—the girl I had a crush on for years. I finally worked up enough courage to ask her to go to the prom, and she said yes. Today was going to be the day that she fell madly in love with me.

We were eating suckers in the car, and after I

finished mine, I was left holding that sticky, paper stick. It was all slobbery and gross. So, I decided to let it fly out of the window. I placed it between my fingers, put my hand on top of the glass, and the rushing air did the rest, sucking it right out of my fingers.

I pulled my hand down and continued to listen to the music, when all of a sudden I heard, "*I can't believe you just did that!*" My date glared at me with a piercing stare so harsh it could burn a hole through the sun. I swallowed and, stammering, tried to explain that the stick was made from paper and was biodegradable.

It was too late. I couldn't take it back. The damage was done; the girl of my dreams was now disgusted by me, the litterer. I may as well have dumped crude oil on a baby seal. I was finished. In the eyes of my dream date, I was a dirty scoundrel.

The rest of the day was fantastic … NOT!

Living Large:

Have you ever done something you truly wish you could take back? The great thing about God's forgiveness is that even though we may do stupid things, God still forgives us.

If you feel guilty about something you have done, pause and pray. Ask God to forgive you for it and then believe that He has forgiven you.

Day 28

Pro-choice

(Not What You Think)

Love is patient, love is kind and is not jealous;
love does not brag and is not arrogant, does not
act unbecomingly; it does not seek its own, is not
provoked, does not take into account a wrong
suffered, does not rejoice in unrighteousness, but
rejoices with the truth; bears all things, believes
all things, hopes all things, endures all things.
Love never fails.

1 Corinthians 13:4-8

It's quite possible that your life has been affected by divorce. I saw somewhere that the statistics for the United States are that one in every two marriages ends in divorce.

Divorce bothers me. What bothers me the most are the excuses that people make to explain their divorce. People say, for example, "I just woke up one morning and realized I didn't love him/her anymore." That's baloney!

Love is a choice; it is not a feeling. Love is a choice that you make every single moment of every single day of your entire life. You choose who you love and how you love them.

Lust is a feeling, not love. When people say that they woke up one morning and didn't love the other person, they are actually saying they didn't "lust" after that person anymore. Their confession is that they're bored with their mate. When people base their relationships on lust and attraction, rather than choosing to love someone daily, those relationships die.

When we lust after something, whether it's a person, food, or entertainment, we eventually get bored with it. I can't tell you how many times I've dropped a video game into my Xbox 360—a game that I absolutely *loved* playing, a game that I would spend all of my free time playing—and then one day it would happen. I would insert the game only to find out I didn't love that game anymore. I was bored with it. I needed to find something new and different to give me that same feeling of love I had with the other game.

Some of the best marriages in the world are arranged marriages. In an arranged marriage, each person has to learn to love the other person. They have to choose to love the other person every moment of every day. I have heard people who have arranged marriages talk about how they had to learn to love the other person and how they went from complete strangers on their wedding day to having a deep love for each other.

Living Large:

Romantic love is a choice that we make over and over again. It is a choice that surpasses boredom and lust. It is a *commitment* to the other person that you will *choose* to love them through the good and bad times. Do you think you are ready to love someone? Are you ready to commit your whole life and future to them?

God is the greatest example when it comes to love. Despite all of mankind's stupidity throughout history, God still loves us. He is committed. He has chosen again and again to love us through it all. What greater example do we need?

It is good to recognize that you are not ready to marry someone just yet. Make a list of the areas in your life that you need to mature in so you can become a man or a woman who is ready for marriage one day.

Day 29

Don't Break the Yoke

*Do not be bound together with unbelievers;
for what partnership have righteousness and
lawlessness, or what fellowship has light with
darkness? Or what harmony has Christ with
Belial, or what has a believer in common
with an unbeliever? Or what agreement has
the temple of God with idols? For we are the
temple of the living God; just as God said,
"I will dwell in them and walk among them;
And I will be their God, and they shall be My
people."*

2 Corinthians 6:14-16

We covered that love is a choice, and hopefully you understand that. When it comes to romantic love, there is another very important concept. We, as Christians, are not to be yoked to unbelievers.

Basically, a yoke is a tool that connects two oxen together. When the oxen walk, they walk in unison.

The Bible says that we need to walk in unison with believers. Pretty simple concept, right?

Wrong! So many people mess this up. This refers to marriage and dating—not just marriage, as many people try to say. When you are dating *and* when you are married, you are yoked to the other person. You are taking your lives in the same direction. Your concerns are tied to each other. You are traveling the same path in life. You are yoked.

As Christians, we need to be equally yoked by dating and marrying other Christians. The reason is simple. It's so you can have the best life possible. You need to find someone who is committed to choose to love you every moment of every day for the rest of your life. You want the person with whom you are yoked to value you and your spiritual journey as much as their own. You want them to love you as Christ loves the church.

I'll give you an example. I have a friend who is still a very good friend. She is beautiful and fun to be with. I met her in college, and we have been great friends ever since. There were many times in college when I thought about trying to turn our friendship into something more romantic, and many times I thought she felt the same way.

We got along great, but there was one major problem. We wouldn't have been equally yoked. We saw differently on everything from politics to religion. Eventually, these major differences would have caught up with us, and we would have fought all the time. It would have torn our relationship apart and we would have lost our friendship. If we had gotten married, we probably would have ended up miserable or divorced.

On the flip side is my relationship with my wife.

We agree on a lot. We have the same beliefs and the same commitment to Jesus. My wife is beautiful, and we have so much in common. We are equally yoked, and it's easy to travel the same path with her. I know that every day she will wake up and choose to love me every moment of that day, no matter how big a jerk I am at times. And she knows I will do the same with her.

Living Large:

The Bible tells us to be equally yoked, not because it's easy or perfect, but because it's the best chance that we will find a love that will last. What characteristics do you think that you will want to see in your future spouse? Begin praying that one day God will lead you to recognize these characteristics in a wonderful, godly woman.

Day 30

I Wish We'd All Been Ready

But according to His promise we are looking for
new heavens and a new earth,
in which righteousness dwells.

2 Peter 3:13

One summer at church camp, during my junior high years, I learned about the rapture. The rapture is the event in history, which is yet to come, where God takes the living believers to heaven. Only God knows the exact time or details.

I learned about the rapture from a movie made in the 1970s. In the movie, all believers disappear. Cars crash when the drivers disappear, and people vanish right out of their clothes. This movie messed me up for years.

Every time I woke up and couldn't find the rest of my family, I freaked out. I searched the house for them, and if I couldn't find them, I called all their phone numbers. I checked the garage for vehicles. It was freaky! There would be other times when I woke up and no one was home, but the cars were in the garage. I checked my parents' bed for clothes to see if they had vanished out of them. But, I knew that the rapture wasn't an exact science; their clothes could have gone with them.

My final effort to figure out if I had been left in the rapture would be to turn the television on and check the news. I knew that the news stations would have to do an emergency story if all the Christians had suddenly disappeared.

The crazy thing about my rapture fear is that I was a Christian kid. This movie just made me paranoid. My advice: don't watch this movie or any like it. It will mess with your mind! Wait to watch rapture movies until you understand more about your faith and have had some pastoral instruction on the rapture.

Living Large:

Devoted Christians should not fear the rapture. We should be excited about the possibility of it happening during our lifetime. Nothing will be greater than going to heaven without facing earthly death. I have great excitement about being called home to heaven to meet Jesus face to face. I hope you share in this excitement.

The rapture may never occur in our lifetime, and we have 2,000-plus years of history in which it hasn't happened. I don't live each day as if the rapture is imminent; I just try to live each day in relationship with Jesus. If I do that, then I know that my eternity will take care of itself. I encourage you to do the same.

If today was the day Jesus came back to take all the Christians to heaven, would that include you? If your answer is no, what can you do to correct that right now?

About the Author:

Cyle Young lives in Youngstown, Ohio and is the Senior Editor of iBegat.com, a website devoted to teens. Cyle is currently serving at Old North Church in Canfield, Ohio. He has worked with teens and children for fifteen years as a Youth Pastor, Children's Pastor, and Youth Summer Camp Director. He loves to be crazy and relishes life; his has been very colorful and adventurous. He also enjoys making people laugh and talking about Jesus. Check out Cyle's website at: www.cyleyoung.com.

Cyle is married to his wonderful wife of seven years, Patty. He has one crazy little red-headed son, Carver, one princess, Cyleigh-Anne, and one happy-all-the-time son, Carrick. He has also lost two children, Peace and Payton. You can learn about Cyle's daughters at: www.peacebears.org. Cyle is also a graduate of The University of Michigan and Liberty Theological Seminary.

CPSIA information can be obtained
at www.ICGtesting.com
Printed in the USA
FFOW02n0626041113
2232FF

9 781938 499975